Samuel French Acting Edition

Lillian

by David Cale

SAMUELFRENCH.COM   SAMUELFRENCH.CO.UK

Copyright © 2019 by David Cale
All Rights Reserved

LILLIAN is fully protected under the copyright laws of the United States of America, the British Commonwealth, including Canada, and all other countries of the Copyright Union. All rights, including professional and amateur stage productions, recitation, lecturing, public reading, motion picture, radio broadcasting, television and the rights of translation into foreign languages are strictly reserved.

ISBN 978-0-573-70729-2

www.SamuelFrench.com
www.SamuelFrench.co.uk

FOR PRODUCTION ENQUIRIES

UNITED STATES AND CANADA
Info@SamuelFrench.com
1-866-598-8449

UNITED KINGDOM AND EUROPE
Plays@SamuelFrench.co.uk
020-7255-4302

Each title is subject to availability from Samuel French, depending upon country of performance. Please be aware that *LILLIAN* may not be licensed by Samuel French in your territory. Professional and amateur producers should contact the nearest Samuel French office or licensing partner to verify availability.

CAUTION: Professional and amateur producers are hereby warned that *LILLIAN* is subject to a licensing fee. Publication of this play(s) does not imply availability for performance. Both amateurs and professionals considering a production are strongly advised to apply to Samuel French before starting rehearsals, advertising, or booking a theatre. A licensing fee must be paid whether the title(s) is presented for charity or gain and whether or not admission is charged. Professional/Stock licensing fees are quoted upon application to Samuel French.

No one shall make any changes in this title(s) for the purpose of production. No part of this book may be reproduced, stored in a retrieval system, or transmitted in any form, by any means, now known or yet to be invented, including mechanical, electronic, photocopying, recording, videotaping, or otherwise, without the prior written permission of the publisher. No one shall upload this title(s), or part of this title(s), to any social media websites.

For all enquiries regarding motion picture, television, and other media rights, please contact Samuel French.

MUSIC USE NOTE

Licensees are solely responsible for obtaining formal written permission from copyright owners to use copyrighted music in the performance of this play and are strongly cautioned to do so. If no such permission is obtained by the licensee, then the licensee must use only original music that the licensee owns and controls. Licensees are solely responsible and liable for all music clearances and shall indemnify the copyright owners of the play(s) and their licensing agent, Samuel French, against any costs, expenses, losses and liabilities arising from the use of music by licensees. Please contact the appropriate music licensing authority in your territory for the rights to any incidental music.

IMPORTANT BILLING AND CREDIT REQUIREMENTS

If you have obtained performance rights to this title, please refer to your licensing agreement for important billing and credit requirements.

LILLIAN premiered at the Goodman Studio Theatre (Robert Falls, Artistic Director; Roche Schulfer, Executive Director) in Chicago, Illinois on October 27, 1997.

LILLIAN subsequently opened Off-Broadway at Playwrights Horizons (Tim Sanford, Artistic Director) in June 1998, with the same artistic team. The director was Joe Mantello, with sets by Robert Brill and lights by Beverly Emmons. The cast was as follows:

LILLIAN. . . . . David Cale

CHARACTERS

LILLIAN – an English woman in her early forties

Part One

The Present

CHRYSANTHEMUMS

Stage is bare except for a stool, a microphone, and a small wooden table with a vase of yellow chrysanthemums and a glass of water.

Lillian enters holding a single yellow bloom.

She stands at the microphone.

Chrysanthemums are considered to be late bloomers. Originating in China, they date back as far as five hundred years B.C. The wild native version of the species has now almost disappeared. Having been completely overshadowed by its more colorful domesticated relative. For optimum results chrysanthemums require a clay soil, a sunny yet cool location, ideally facing south, and loam. They are what's known as short-day plants, meaning they are light sensitive and produce buds only as the days become shorter and the nights grow longer. To improve the quality of the flowers the first bud that appears should be pinched, that's according to most chrysanthemum experts, in whose ranks I now number myself, thereby increasing the radiance of the subsequent flowers.

She places the bloom on the stool.

The other day I overheard a landscape gardener talking to a woman I know who designs plaster gnomes to put on your front lawn: a garden ornament whose appeal has frankly always eluded me. Anyway the landscape gardener says,

"I realized recently that I have been mildly depressed for the last fifteen years."

The gnome lady asks,
"How come you only realize that now?"
He answered,
"Because I don't feel that way anymore."
It's funny what you just happen to overhear.

I wonder if it's true that all the secrets of our lives are whispered into our ears at birth. That the secrets then attach themselves to our unconscious. As years pass occasionally a secret will break free, and make its way up into our daily thoughts. They are then referred to as premonitions. I think we know everything that's going to happen to us.

People come into your life for a reason. There are no accidents. There's nothing haphazard about it. Or coincidental. What may seem random at the time, I think in the end has a kind of correctness.

She picks up the flower.

I mean, in retrospect, when you look back on your life, if you're able to be honest with yourself, I think you come to realize, it could not have happened any other way.

Lights fade. Lillian places the bloom in the vase.

Part Two

Seven Years Earlier

THIS JIMMY THING

Lillian is seated on the stool.

"The thought of someone else inside you is something I could never come to terms with,"
Keith had said to me before he went up north on that job.
"I could get over somebody kissing you, or cuddling, but if anyone went inside, I don't think I could ever touch you again."
"Don't be dramatic," I'd said.
"No one's going anywhere with me."

Then almost the minute the door shut.
Keith was hardly in his precious Volvo,
when I meet little Jimmy in the store,
fifteen years my junior,
with a look on his face that could drag a shipwreck up from the bottom of the ocean.

"Wipe that dirty look off your face, Jimmy Foyle," I said,
"and stop trying to put your fingers in my mouth,
I'm a married woman."

I couldn't believe the words were coming out of me.
It was like my husband just flew out the window.

A Jimmy was really what I had in mind for a lover before I met Keith. He was the kind of person I always wanted when I was his age, but who never seemed interested in me. I wasn't generally a Jimmy's type. Jimmys didn't generally, give women like me a second look. We seemed too tame. Jimmy was a wild one. Rough around the edges. He was bit of a devil. Didn't give things a lot of thought the way Keith did. And he was funny. Keith had nothing approaching a sense of humor. Actually Keith was the only person I knew that didn't find me funny in any way.

"I can't believe that, Lillian," Jimmy said. "You're a riot."
How refreshing, I thought, to be found funny again.

It was really the idea of a Jimmy coming along that kept me from completely giving over to Keith. I'd been holding out for the thought of a Jimmy for a long time. So when he aimed his eyes at me and came on so strong that day, something in me was saying, "It would not be a good idea to turn Jimmy down. It'll be a little fling. You have to work out this Jimmy thing. Lillian, it's between you and yourself."

Jimmy knew Keith was out of town. I think he'd even been watching the precious Volvo to see if it was still in the front. He invited me to come over to his house to see his lizards.

"Lizards?" I said.

"Yes," he said.

"How peculiar," I said. "Alright, Jimmy."

He drove his car like he'd just robbed a bank. We ran a red light.

Hold onto your seat, Lillian, I thought. His car didn't have safety belts.

"I cut them off," he said. "They were uncomfortable."

I thought about Keith. Keith wouldn't start the engine unless everyone was strapped in.

Jimmy's house was lined with tiny aquariums. He got all excited as he told me what the various lizards were and where they came from. He was quite the authority.

Outside of the store he looked much younger.

God, Lillian, I thought, what are you doing?

When he made his move on me it was so sudden. Talk about a pounce. Even the lizards scuttled behind their plastic rocks. I immediately felt like I'd been thrown into a wrestling ring. As we were rolling around on his leopard blanket, I must confess my first thought was, am I really enjoying this?

He was so rough, and young. There was no warming up with Jimmy. In fact, much to my surprise, it was dreadful. It's funny, I realized I'd gotten used to Keith's mouth. Jimmy had a smaller mouth. I think Keith's tongue was wider too. There was nothing sensual about Jimmy's tongue. It just sort of flickered around in my mouth, like the tongues of one of those lizards of his.

Whatever was wrong with Keith, the sexual part was alright.

Or maybe I'd over-rated it a bit. But he was considerate. Sexually speaking I'd say Keith was like a really good waiter in a pretty good restaurant. Very good service, but ultimately disappointing food. Jimmy seemed to approach the whole thing like it was some form of Kung Fu, or that I was something that needed to be overthrown, but really I was just laying there. He was nervous, bless him. I tried to get him to ease up.

"Slow down," I said, in a voice that was supposed to sound seductive, but I have to admit did come out rather motherly.

"If I slow down," he said, "I'll lose the erection."

God, I thought, this is dreadful, as he's pulling my sweater over my chin.

Then he breathed into my ear,

"Can I fuck you, Lillian?"

And I thought about Keith and what the thought of somebody else being inside me would do to him, and how it really would be the final straw and I said,

"Yes Jimmy, if you want."

He got all excited and ran into another room. Came back with a Rubber Johnny, and he had trouble opening the packet. And I'm thinking, if I let Jimmy inside, then there's no going back.

He lays back down on top and I put my hand on the erection he was so afraid of losing, which I realized I hadn't even looked at yet, so I took a peek.

Oh dear, I thought, men's penises are all starting to look the same, as I helped it find it's way inside.

"Is it in?" Jimmy said. He was nervous, bless him.

"Yes, it's in," I said.

Jimmy takes this as his cue to start pounding away at me with his eyes scrunched shut.

Christ look at me, I thought.

I hate it when men shut their eyes and lock off into their own world.

"You're in my world now," I felt like saying.

And I'm thinking of Keith on that oil rig. Wish Keith had gotten more excited about doing things. We should have gone on holidays. Little adventures. It was such a routine. Wish Keith would get all riled up. Wish he'd get passionate about something. Oh I don't know, about life, or me, or lose his temper.

"You know I love you," he'd say, "I don't need to keep telling you. I wouldn't dream of looking at another woman."

And he wouldn't.

And I'm looking at Jimmy's lizards. Can they really be happy in those little tanks with a light bulb over their heads morning and night? And I look at Jimmy on top of me, and his face looks like it's in such pain. His eyes are still squeezed tight. There's sweat forming on his forehead. And he took so long. God I wish he'd have his orgasm and this could be over. It's starting to feel like a visit to the dentist's, more than a sexual fling. Then Jimmy makes a noise like he's been shot in the leg, and I realize (thank God), he's having his little eruption, bless him.

He rolls over to the other side of the blanket.

"That was sexy," he says.

"Yes," I said, "it was very. Thank you."

Oh Lillian, polite to the end.

But then Jimmy did some really sweet things. He ran a bath. Put something blue in the water. He showed me his muscles.

"Oooh," I said.

He lit candles. He was quite romantic after all. He was a boy really. I half expected the police to come barging in and arrest me.

"Did I disappoint you?" he said.

"No, of course not," I said.

And for a moment he looked so vulnerable that I thought my heart would break.

We sat in the bath. He was behind me. He did my back.

Drew objects on my shoulders in soap and had me guess what they were.

"It's a giraffe," I said.

"No, it's a crane," he said.

"You win," I said.

He was laughing.

He looked even younger with his hair wet. He has lovely olive eyes. I didn't realize till we were in the water lit by the birthday candles, bless him. One day some young woman's going to really lose her bearings just looking into those eyes, I thought. And I got a little rush of sadness, but not anything so big that it would register on my face.

He dried me with a fresh towel. He fixed a snack. We watched the tele. He had his hand on my thigh. He asked,

"How does your pussy feel?"

I said,

"What did you say?"

He said,

"You heard me."

I said,

"That's for me to know, and you to imagine.
Cheeky bugger."

I smiled. He laughed.

"Oh Lillian, you're a riot," he said, for the second time.

What could I say?

"Actually I'm in distinct discomfort."

It would have broken his heart, bless him.

And he was playing with the nape of my neck with his fingers, and it was tickling me in a sort of irritating way, but I didn't say anything.

And one of Jimmy's lizards is watching us with a large cricket in its mouth, which it's in the process of crunching on. The cricket's antennae are waving slowly as its body disappears.

And I'm thinking of Keith in his Volvo, following the tail lights of another car, with his radio on. He was probably near Scotland by then. With that perpetually anxious look on his face, that he inherited from his father. And Jimmy's giggling at a commercial on the television.

Looking all of sixteen.

And they're both nice men. Sweet men. You know, good people. And as the damn television is chattering away in the background, all I can think is,

Well my dear, now what?

Lights fade.

Part Three
Five Years Later

BRIGHTON

Lillian is seated on the stool.

When I was young my school reports all said the same thing: "She has potential, but she has a tendency to procrastinate." I didn't know what the word meant. Neither did my mother. She was always saying,
"I must buy a dictionary tomorrow and look up that word."

That little memory has always nagged at me for some reason. That, and memories of Brighton.

I've always felt a special bond with Brighton. I used to go there as a child. My grandfather had a place. In Hove, to be more precise. Hove is literally next door. They're right side by side. But some people get quite upset if you confuse them. "The working people go to Brighton," my grandfather would say, as if he didn't work. "This family is on it's way to Hove." It's so silly really.

On the train down I found myself becoming quite reflective. Keith used to say I spent too much time with my head in the past, and he was probably right.

"Don't dwell," he'd say. "The past is gone."
And he'd bark out the word "gone."

Riding trains always makes me reflective. I'm sure it's all those sights passing you by at such speed does it. My ex-husband hadn't crossed my mind in a long time but for some reason I found myself thinking about him on the train to Brighton. One thing that's always stayed with me about Keith was the way he'd say, "I know that one day you'll leave." I'd tell him not to think like that, but I knew he was right. Deep down. The moment I met Keith I imagined myself saying goodbye to him.

LILLIAN

I'd been working in a bookstore in London for six months, which I did quite enjoy. It was a comfortable position. Civilized kind of customer. There were many days when it didn't seem like work. I've always liked being around books. It's funny, I rarely read them, I just like being in their presence. As if at any point you could pick one up, open it and enhance yourself. I don't know why I won't read. It's as if part of me has always shied away from the idea of any kind of enhancement. It's made all the more peculiar by the fact that I buy books all the time. My house is lined with unread books.

Anyway, I had decided to take a week off work. It was drizzling in London. February. The store was quiet. Brighton will be empty this time of year, I thought. Time to take some time to re-charge. Soon as I get out of the train station there I always feel a sense of both relief and release. Oh the times I've gotten on a train and run back to Brighton.

I'd been there for about a day and a half and it was really doing the trick. There were very few people on the street. Felt like I had the place to myself.

Well I was walking along the front, past the chalets on the beach, when I hear somebody calling my name. I turn around and see this young man with a beard waving at me. Who on earth are you? I thought, and presumed it must be a customer from the shop.

"It's me," said the man with the beard, "it's Jimmy. Don't you remember?"

"Jimmy!" I said, totally taken aback. "You look completely different. I would have walked right past you."

Besides the beard he was much slimmer, and it's probably my imagination but I think he'd grown.

"What are you doing here?" I asked.

"I live here," he said.

"Since when?"

"Since about four years ago."

I couldn't get over how different he looked.

"I don't lift weights anymore," he said, "I do Tai Chi. Lost a lot of bulk. Don't have the muscles anymore. And I've gone vegetarian."

"And you have the beard now," I chimed in.

"Yeah, my wife says it gives me authority."

"Your wife!" I said.

"Can you believe it?" he said, "I got hitched."

The whole episode was quite disorienting. Having Jimmy pop up in the middle of my Brighton, after how many years? Five was it? He asked me if I'd like to grab a bite. Said I would. I have to say it was immediately comfortable between us. One thing about Jimmy and I, we always got along.

"I don't drink coffee anymore," he said. "Only herb tea. I'm watching my health. But I could have a chamomile tea and a tofu sandwich. I'm very strict."

"Tofu sandwich!" I said. "Oh dear. I shall be having a glass of wine, a pastry, a cappuccino and a cigarette. In that order. Health kick!"

He laughed.

Oh good, I thought, I'm still amusing to him.

While he wasn't looking I glanced at the side of his face. He'd become quite beautiful. Delicate almost. In the looks department, I have to say, the little bugger had really come into his own.

We went to an awful "health" restaurant where they had a lot of attitude and no pastry and when I tried to light a cigarette I got a lecture on second-hand smoke. He wanted me to meet his wife. Thought the two of us would get along. Why? I couldn't help wondering.

"She reminds me of you," he said. "She's a bit older than me. Very successful in business. Has her own company. I work for her. She trains executives how to speak in public, and how to alter their image so they'll become a more effective tool in the marketplace."

The whole enterprise sounded positively creepy. I asked him what his role in all this was. He said he videotaped the executives speaking and that "Donna" – the wife, would identify their weaknesses, and therefore help to rectify them.

"How old are you now?" I asked, somewhat shifting the subject.

"Twenty-six," he said. "How old are you?"

"I'm not telling you how old I am," I said. "Let's put it this way, when I write down my date of birth now, I put the word circa next to it."

Then he asked if I thought he seemed more mature. Apparently Donna was working on having him project a more mature version of himself.

"Have you noticed I'm speaking slower?" he said. "Donna got me to do that. She made me watch a video of myself. I had no idea I talked so quickly."

I'd never noticed it.

Poor Jimmy was starting to sound a bit like someone who's had a complete nervous breakdown and who's slowly pasting themselves back together. And I was gaining the impression he'd married Eva Braun.

She's not pointing any cameras at me, I thought.

Just as some horrendous-looking alfalfa something-or-other arrived, he asked me how what's-his-name was.

"If you mean Keith," I said, "I have no idea. I haven't seen Keith for nearly two years. Last time I tried to talk to Keith he said he still wasn't ready to speak to me yet."

"Was it because of me?" he asked, with a tone of slight self-satisfaction. And I have to say it did irritate me for a moment. I mean there was a reason I stayed with Keith for six years. It wasn't a complete waste of time.

"Let's just say, you didn't help."

One thing about Keith, he could read me like a book. He knew immediately what had happened with Jimmy. "The way you talked about him in the store. It was obvious," he said.

"It's sad," he'd go on, "you're like a little girl. You'll fall for anyone who flatters you."

Keith always referred to Jimmy as "the episode."

"You haven't been the same since the episode," was how he'd put it.

I really didn't want to meet Donna. I imagined her exuding sex appeal and confidence and I really wasn't feeling up to comparisons, but I went along with it. For some reason Jimmy was so eager for us to meet. He called her up. Warned her we were on our way, while I excused myself to go to the bathroom, for an emergency one-on-one between myself and my face in the bathroom mirror. I hope it's the light in here, I thought. Either that, my dear, or it's time to lay off the lattes.

Donna was on a business call when we walked in. With her back to us. She was nothing at all like I'd anticipated. Donna was a big girl. Literally. She must have been at least 6'2" and I have to say, and this will sound awfully ungenerous on my part, and it is, but the first thing that drew my attention were her hips. She's probably given birth to something, I presumed. When she turned around I thought, oh I'm much better looking than you, and I was sort of surprised at myself for how juvenile I was behaving. But I have to say I did suddenly feel in the mood to be a little...oh, I don't know, yes I do...threatening.

Finally, she gets off the phone. Waltzes over, extending her hand.

"I'm sorry," she says, "the Americans just think I've got all the time in the world. But they're where the money is, so we can't be complaining too much, now can we?"

Then she kissed Jimmy on the mouth in front of me, which seemed a bit unnecessary, and said, "Hello, James." James! I thought, James! Well, excuse me! Jimmy may have been many things but one thing he wasn't was a James. Redirecting her attention towards me,

"What line are you in Lillian?" she asks.

"Books," I say, "though I seldom read them."

"Oh, publishing?" she says.

"No," says I, "secondhand mostly."

"Oh," she says.

"What a pretty shirt you're wearing."

And I thought,

You cow!

I was only there for about ten minutes, which was quite long enough. Donna said she had a meeting to go to.

"Oh, A.A.?" I inquired.

"Oh you're hilarious," she says.

"So are you," I replied.

Which got no response.

She said she was going to Germany for the rest of the week for a conference, and that "James" had the car. Every time she mentioned "James" I had to think for a moment who she was talking about.

"You two can get re-acquainted," she said. "You don't need me around now, do you?" And for a second it felt like she was throwing him at me.

Jimmy wanted to give me a tour of the south coast, so the following day, after Donna left, he picked me up at the hotel and we went driving in her BMW.

"What happened to your car?" I asked.

"Donna made me get rid of it," he said.

"I liked that car!" I protested. "It suited you."

"She approves of you," he said. "She thought you were down to earth."

Which from a pretentious person is not a compliment.

"She thinks you're the kind of woman that she could imagine me being with much more than her."

"What does she mean by that?" I asked.

"I don't know," he said. "Sometimes I think she's tired of being married to people. I'm her fourth husband."

"Oh," I said, and then we just drove for a bit without saying anything. The countryside along the south coast is lovely. And I remembered how much I liked to be in the passenger seat of a car.

While Jimmy was driving I happened to notice his hands on the steering wheel. They looked older. I looked at mine. I'm sure they did too. He slipped in a CD.

> *A romantic, propulsive pop/rock song begins to play in the car.* The song underscores the following seven lines.*

I lowered my window. A gust of wind blew through the car. My hair went everywhere. Care and all its relatives seemed to fall out of me. Well I don't know if it was the sea air, the music, too many cappuccinos or Jimmy. But I felt a sudden wave of enthusiasm. He must have thought my mind had just fluttered out the car window.

"Right now," I exclaimed, "I feel like I'm riding the world!"

> *Music crescendos and plays at a louder volume for thirty seconds then returns to the original level to underscore the next three lines.*

---

*A license to produce *Lillian* does not include a performance license for any third-party or copyrighted music. Licensees should create an original composition or use music in the public domain. For further information, please see Music Use Note on page 3.

Driving along the coast we came to a huge fun fair. Jimmy wanted to get off the road and investigate. I didn't take much convincing. As we were going in he stopped in his tracks.

Music ends.

"I always get excited around you," he said.

"I feel the same way," I told him.

And I realized what it was: you see you could be romantic with Jimmy and not feel like a fool. I'd been waiting a long time to be romantic with someone.

Jimmy was immediately drawn to an enormous roller coaster called The Big Plunge. The Big Plunge was a ride that would go up extremely high and then plummet.

Now I have a terrible fear of heights. "There's no way you're going to get me up on that thing," I said. "You go if you want to. I'll stay here and have a cigarette."

"Oh Lillian, you're afraid of everything," he said.

"How dare you!" I said, "I am not."

"Come on," he said. "Fear at a certain point just becomes another bad habit."

Which had to have been something he'd picked up from Donna.

The only way I could go on The Big Plunge was by going through a complicated psychological snow job in which I rationalized that my fear of heights actually represented my terror of life, and that going on The Big Plunge was extremely important for me and could lead to a personal breakthrough. Besides if ten-year-old children could brave it, so could I. Jimmy managed to grab the front seat.

"I'm sure I'm the oldest person to ever take the plunge," I said, ever the terrified wit, as the ride yanked everyone forward and the squealing began.

LILLIAN

First off I was petrified and then I seemed to push through the fear, and I have to say the whole thing did seem like a personal breakthrough. Donna would have been proud of me. Jimmy held my hand for the duration, which was sweet of him. I've never been able to go on those rides before but I ended up loving it, and went on three more times.

It had become completely easy between us and midway through the day a strange notion crossed my mind.

I can imagine myself being with you for a long time, I thought.

By late afternoon I realized I really was getting a little lightheaded around Jimmy. I stood at a distance as he was buying tickets for the next ride. Tried to give myself a little talking-to.

"He's twenty-six. He's married. He lives in Brighton," I said to myself, "Lillian, stop it!"

Then out of the blue on the Ferris wheel he gave me a peck on the cheek.

"What are you doing?" I asked, trying not to sound delighted, and failing abysmally.

"I wanted to kiss you," he said.

"James," I scolded, "behave!"

The Ferris wheel then abruptly jolted to a halt.

Fortunately, with us on the low end.

While we were waiting to move, Jimmy asked what seemed to be an out-of-the-blue question.

"If somebody told you your life would end in, say a year, do you think you'd start to really live? Or do you think you'd slip back under the covers and wait for it to be over?"

"I think I'd get a move on," I replied.

Just then the wheel began to turn.

As we were passing the arcade I noticed a photo booth.

"I don't have any pictures of you," I said. "Come on, I need some proof that you exist."

We were clowning around in front of the camera. Pictures took forever to come out. When they finally did emerge from the machine I wasn't quite prepared for what I saw. What took me back about the photos was that we looked like two people who were completely in love with each other. I'm sure Jimmy picked up on it too. But neither of us said anything.

Driving back to my hotel I started to feel uneasy. I asked him if he wanted to come up to the room for a bit. Dangling the fact that there was a good-sized color TV. I had forgotten how small the room was and it did feel a little awkward. There was nowhere to sit except the bed.

"We have quite a history," I said.

"Yes," he agreed.

"You and me."

Placing his hand on my ankle.

"Your leg feels swollen," he said.

I told him it was the circulation. That my varicose veins were getting worse. Then regretted drawing attention to them. Tried to make a joke.

"I'm not supposed to ever cross my legs again."

"Can't they take them out?" he asked.

"The doctor said it would be for purely cosmetic reasons to remove them," I replied, "and he strongly advised against it."

"Oh," he said, and then went quiet and seemed withdrawn.

"What about wearing a special stocking?"

"Please stop talking about varicose veins. They don't exactly make me feel like an attractive proposition."

"Are you alright?" I asked.

He didn't say anything. He just nodded. Then I don't know what triggered it exactly but he just started sobbing.

"I fucked up my life," he said.

"What's wrong?" I asked him.

"I wanted to be married to someone. I wanted to make it work. Wanted a family. Didn't want to be like my old man. I hate my life. I want to be a gardener. Want to have a nursery and grow things. I don't want to be videotaping businessmen all day. I hate that world. I want to be outside. Donna says she's not willing to be married to a gardener. She wants to have an open relationship. Wants to be able to see other people. I know she's seeing someone in Germany. She doesn't love me, she just likes showing me off to her girlfriends. 'Cause I'm young. They call me the puppy. You should hear them. 'Did you toilet train the puppy yet?' 'Oh Donna, the puppy's so cute.'"

"Come on," I said, "stop crying. You've got me going now." And I started up.

"Look at the two of us. We're downright unstable."

"Oh, Lillian," he cried.

"Come here," I said and put my arms around him. He felt like a different person without the muscles. With that damn beard. He felt like a stranger.

"My Jimmy," I said.

And I don't know what possessed me but I really wanted to kiss him. Even though he was distraught and fragile-seeming, and it was probably most inappropriate. I wanted to push through that to his mouth. So I did. And he didn't pull away, and for a second I thought about Donna, and that I didn't want to go where her lips had been, but then I dismissed that, and I kissed him again. And it was a long kiss. The kind of kiss you could never get bored of. The kind of kiss you could re-discover yourself inside. And it was so tender and unguarded between us, and I knew I was falling and I did nothing to catch myself. It felt like a dam was opening in my chest, and all these feelings that I'd been waiting for years to put into motion, were flooding my entire insides. And I could have had the good sense to get up or ask him to leave, and the dam would have surely blocked, but instead I just let it all come crashing down.

On the train back from Brighton the following day, I stared out of the window for almost the entire ride. Couldn't tell you if the train was crowded or if there was even anyone sitting next to me. I took out the strip of photos we'd taken in the booth. Examined them. As we came into London, the conductor approached and said to me,

"Don't leave anything behind."

I said,

"What did you say?"

Even though I heard him the first time.

He said,

"Don't leave anything behind."

I put the photos in my bag. I looked at him. He smiled. I smiled.

"I won't," I said, "I won't leave anything behind."

Lights dip and then come back up sharply.

Part Four

Two Hours Later

OUT OF BREATH

Lillian is seated on the stool.

When I walked in the door the phone was ringing.

I dropped everything. Ran for the receiver. It was an out-of-breath Jimmy.

"I want to be with you," he says.

"I want you.

I never said that to anyone before.

I'm leaving Donna.

She gets back tomorrow.

I'm telling her tomorrow.

But first I need to check.

Do you want to be with me?"

And he suddenly struck me as so young, and a little desperate, but I said,

"Yes, I do."

I said,

"Yes, I do,"

anyway.

Lights fade.

Part Five

One Year Later

THERE YOU GO

Lillian is standing. Sipping from the glass of water.

I've always felt like somewhat of a mystery to myself. As if there were whole territories inside me that existed beyond the grasp of my comprehension. I love having so much inside remain unknown. That's why I've always distrusted psychoanalysis. To me, at a certain point, it eats away a person's mystery.

"That's not mystery, that's pain," say my friends.

Seemed like everyone I knew was trying to explain themselves.

"What about instinct? Gut feeling?" I'd say.

When I die they'll find intuition at the wheel. With probably fear still sitting in the back seat trying to bark out directions. But intuition at the wheel.

"Be warned, Lillian. The way you got him will be the way you lose him," was the general consensus of most of the over-psychoanalyzed people I knew.

"He's a lost and broken boy, and you're not his mother."

She places the glass on the stool next to her.

When I married Jimmy no one was invited.

"Don't you want anyone to give you away?" he asked.

To which I replied that I would be giving myself away this time, thank you very much.

We were married in a registrar's office by a man whose accent was so thick that to this day I'm not completely clear what I was agreeing to. Not wishing to appear rude by asking him to repeat everything two or three times, I just basically said yes, yes, yes. There was a plastic cherry blossom tree in each corner of the room, with little fake birds on its branches. Upon closer examination the birds were holding LOVE IS BLIND signs between their bills. Looking closer still I noticed the birds had no eyes. Charming, I thought.

Jimmy showed up wearing a jacket that can best be described as looking like it had been snatched off the back of a small child who'd been on his way to a birthday party, and he came up with the shadiest looking witness who I had never met before, nor have seen since. I have to say, when I first laid eyes on him I did think to myself, keep your eye on your purse. Nonetheless it was quite the little adventure.

First few months we lived together in London. Jimmy got a job pruning trees for the council. One afternoon I finished up work early, thought, oh I'll take the scenic route home, when by chance, I happened to run into him. He was perched on the main bough of a sycamore. Lopping branches. Huge sections of tree were falling into the road. I called out to him. He looked up sharply.

"Don't do that!" he snapped. "You surprised me."

"That poor tree," I said, "the shock'll kill it."

"You have to be brutal about cutting," he said. "The more you cut away, the better they do. It may seem cruel, but it's for the best. Sometimes you have to nearly kill something before it will grow."

And for a good minute we just stared at each other without saying anything.

Later that day, when he came home from work, he laid down and went to sleep. While he was sleeping I pulled back the covers to look at him. He never wore clothes in bed. Always slept the same way; on his side with his hands covering his face.

Well I noticed something on his heel. I thought, what the hell is that? He had an ant tattooed on his heel, which I'd never noticed before. It was very tiny and very detailed. A quite perfectly proportioned ant.

I laid down next to him, fell asleep myself, and had this dream that Jimmy's back was covered with faint lines. Faint lines and tattooed roads. Winding through freckles. Crisscrossing his backbone. Occasionally passing through a hair. In the dream I asked him what it was. He answered,

"It's a map of your life."

I laughed, "Oh, come on."

He said,

"You started here,"

and he pointed behind himself.

"You're about here now."

And he moved his finger to a place halfway up his back. Over his heart. In the dream I asked him,

"Why does the map end at your shoulder?"

And just as he was about to answer, I woke up.

He had next to nothing in the way of possessions. Everything had belonged to Donna. One of the few things that was actually his was this little tent that he took everywhere. Just in case he ever felt the urge to sleep outside, he'd say.

One Saturday we took a bus ride into the country. Sure enough the little package came along too. No sooner were we off the bus when Jimmy said,

"Let's forget about going home. I wanna sleep under the sky."

I have to say the idea did appeal.

So we bought sandwiches. Supplies. Walked what must have been miles, till we found a spot that met Jimmy's definition of the word remote, by which time the sky was quite black. He set up the little tent and pulled out a sleeping bag that he'd had all along.

By the time we'd eaten it was late and Jimmy was beat so he went pretty much straight to sleep. I, on the other hand, just laid there. The ground was uneven, to put it mildly. I think we were parked on top of a mole community. My spine was wondering what the hell was going on, and it was damp, but I didn't care.

It was so quiet in the open. You could almost hear your moods change. If you laid still enough you could feel your instincts wriggling to the surface.

Hours go by. I'm still wide awake.

Thinking,
I'm forty-one years old.
It's three o'clock in the morning,
and I'm laying in a field.
And the whole thing seemed so absurd, I just started laughing.

You know what, I thought.
Good things are going to happen.
I'm ready for them now. I wasn't before. I am now.
Yes, I thought, I'm ready to roll my sleeves up.
My sleeves are fairly twitching to be rolled.
For the good things.

In the bus on the way back home Jimmy said,
"I can't live without wheels."
But he didn't have two cents to rub together, so I purchased a cheap car. A beaten-up Rover 2000. For a test drive we drove down south to the coast. Just along from Brighton we happened to pass a small cottage for sale with a few acres attached. Four large greenhouses. Quite without thinking I said,
"Pull over, Jimmy."

The place had been a nursery. It required work, that was for sure, but there was something about it that I felt immediately drawn to. I took down the name of the estate agent. Gave them a call, just out of curiosity really, to see what it was going for. Well it was surprisingly inexpensive considering it commanded a good view of the sea and came with a little land. The estate agent told me the woman who lived there before had given birth in the house, and had buried her placenta in the garden. And I thought, why are you telling me this? Oh good, I'll take it. I've been looking for a house with a placenta for the longest time.

I mean really.

But you know, soon as Jimmy and I were inside the place I knew I wanted to live here.

"We could open a nursery." I said.

"You always wanted to do that. I've always had a houseful of plants. At school they called me Green Fingers."

The cottage was empty of furnishings, except on one wall there was an oil painting of two lizards.

"Look lizards!" I cried,

"It's a sign!"

Jimmy didn't say anything. I could sense hesitation but I barreled on. I felt fired up about the idea in a way I'd never felt about any potential vocation. I had some savings tucked away. I did work in a store that had a comprehensive gardening section. On the quiet I made an appointment at my bank to see about obtaining some kind of small business loan. Found it to be surprisingly straightforward.

Then, quite impulsively, without discussion of any kind, I cracked open the nest egg I'd been sitting on, and bought the place.

Everyone I knew was up in arms.

"It's Jimmy's dream, it isn't yours!"

"What are you going to do without your financial cushion? Do you want to end up like some old lady, living on cat food?"

"Oh, for God's sake!" I said.

"This whole episode, and Keith was right, it is an episode, bears a label with the words: 'Tragedy-in-the-making' written all over it," said one person.

"No, you're wrong," I said, "I've been wearing the 'Tragedy-in-the-making' tag around my neck for a long time, and I'm taking it off now."

When it came to packing, I couldn't help thinking about Jimmy cutting that tree and I was ruthless.
"I'll just take my book collection and only what I like.
The past is gone," I said, "I'm not dragging it around anymore."

I just walked away from London and my life there.

"I'll get fresh friends," I thought. "I'll start new."

As we were driving down the motorway I felt as though I were on the run from the law, but Jimmy didn't say a word. Didn't play music. Just stared straight ahead.

I asked him,

"What's wrong?"

He said,

"Nothing."

I said,

"Come on, you look like you're on your way to a funeral, or something."

"I don't know anything about you," he said.
"You don't know anything about me.
We're as good as strangers."

"You know me," I said.

And had the strongest feeling that I'd been in this situation before.

Part Six

Same Time

GRACE

Lillian is standing.

We decided the nursery should specialize in chrysanthemums, and Jimmy would do a little landscaping on the side, for extra money. I soon realized it wasn't Brighton that I had loved so much as it was being within close proximity to the sea. From the front of the house, I would find myself transfixed by it.

I love being outside. Getting my hands dirty. Sometimes I'd have to force myself to get up out of the flower beds and call it a day. I'd stand outside in the open sometimes with my arms in the air. The sun in my face. I swear if you could see me from the road, you'd think you'd stumbled across some bizarre cult.

From the moment we moved here though, Jimmy had been acting strangely. We'd have ridiculous petty arguments. Like giving the place a name. He thought we should call it "Lillian's."

"What about you?" I'd say, "Your name?" And he'd argue the place was really mine.

"It's your money. You got the loan. I may as well just work for you."

"It's ours," I'd try to insist. He'd get all sullen, so when customers did start arriving they'd talk to me. They didn't want to deal with him. One night I tried to confront him. To find out what was going wrong. And he barked at me,

"We've become ordinary and I haven't got time to be ordinary!"

I said,

"I thought this is what you wanted."

He counteracted,

"Well maybe I've changed my mind."

I put my arms around him once, to try and comfort him and his body was so tense. It was like holding a piece of wood.

And he wouldn't look me in the eye.

I said,

"Why won't you look at me?"

He said,

"I can't."

I said,

"Why not?"

He said,

"I just can't."

He'd fall asleep on the couch most every night and I couldn't get him to come to bed. Till it became the norm. He would sleep on the couch. The closer the place came to being finished, the more remote it seemed to become between us. We'd go whole mornings without exchanging a word.

One night it was particularly bad. I thought, we can't go on like this. So I said, "I think I should leave for a little bit. I'm going to take the car and go for a drive."

"I didn't know you could drive," Jimmy said.

"I only drive if I have to," I said, "and I think I should go for a drive."

"How long will you be?" he asked.

"How long would you like me to be?"

"A few hours would be good," he said.

"Then I'll go for a few hours.

Aren't you going to say goodbye?"

"Why?" he asked, "We'll see each other again. Won't we?"

And he grinned. And I thought, that's the first time I've seen you smile since we got here.

It felt strange to be at the wheel. Winding through lanes at night. I hadn't driven myself in a long time.
"Where shall we go, Lillian?" I said out loud.
Don't think, I thought, just move.
And I put my foot down.
And for a second I wondered,
Am I dreaming this?

When I came back to the house it was dark. All the lights were turned off. I felt considerably apprehensive about going in. I knew what I'd find. Jimmy was gone. So were his clothes. I knew that would happen. That's why I left the house, so he could leave. You see however bad things got, Jimmy and I understood each other.

But then a strange incident occurred.

> *Cinematic music evoking a kind of mystery begins to play, underscoring the next paragraph.**

I stepped outside the house. Onto the porch. It was pitch-dark. The tall chrysanthemums were in bloom for the first time. The flowers seemed black at night. They were moving slightly. As though something were stirring in them. I heard a noise coming from somewhere in the middle. So I walked into the chrysanthemums. There was a white

---

*A license to produce *Lillian* does not include a performance license for any third-party or copyrighted music. Licensees should create an original composition or use music in the public domain. For further information, please see Music Use Note on page 3.

dog running between the rows. The dog kept turning and looking at me. And every time I'd get close it would start up running again, as though it was leading me somewhere. And I don't know what possessed me but I called out "Jimmy," and the dog stopped in its tracks. Edged towards me. It looked like the kind of dog that no one would want. It licked my hand. For a moment we locked into each other's eyes.

"One day some woman's going to really lose her bearings just looking into those eyes," I said out loud.

And I got a rush of sadness, but it went away. The dog then turned and started running. I called out, "Jimmy," but I didn't call out loud enough. My cry was faint-hearted.

The dog kept going, deeper into the chrysanthemums.

Music fades.

When Jimmy left, my first impulse was to pack up everything and go back to Keith.

When Jimmy left I thought, I can't do it.

When Jimmy left it felt like placing a child in charge of a child.

When Jimmy left I thought,
If you don't begin, you're going to go under.

When Jimmy left I took out the strip of photos we'd taken in the booth, and they were completely blank.

Shortly after Jimmy left, I ran into Donna in London. Actually she came running after me.

"Don't pretend you didn't see me, Lillian," she said.

Oh, Christ, I thought, what do you want?

"Look, I don't think I made a very good impression on you before," she said, "and I'm sorry. To be honest I was going through a kind of therapy at the time which proved quite disastrous. Do you ever hear from our little friend, just out of curiosity?"

I said I hadn't seen "our little friend" for a while, which was true.

"I suppose you know what happened?" she asked.

"I came back from Germany, after your visit, and he was gone. No note. No phone call. No goodbye. No nothing. We were going to move the business back to London, which I did. I live here now. He effectively just disappeared on me. It wasn't working between us. Wouldn't have lasted, he pushed me to marry him, you know."

Then she asked if I knew how his health was.

I said,

"What do you mean?"

She says,

"You know, the heart thing. The arteries are weak, or swollen, I was never quite clear. They could burst at any time. He could flood inside. Frankly," she said, "that's one of the reasons why I was hesitant to marry him. Don't want to set yourself up, do you? Don't mind being a divorcée, but a widow?

Now that ages you."

And she laughed.

"I didn't know him very well," I said. "Let's just say, we helped each other out."

And excused myself to leave.

"How's the publishing business going?" she called out.

"Very well," I said. "Thank you for asking."

I heard from Jimmy once. He sent me a photograph of a woman alone on a beach. Wading in the sea. On the back of the photograph was written:
LILLIAN? Love, Jimmy.
There was no return address.

For about a week I was feeling an inexplicable sadness. Couldn't figure out what it was. When the phone rang I almost didn't answer it. I knew something was up. It was a woman calling from a hospital in West London. She asked me if I knew Jimmy Foyle. I said I did. She said they'd found a piece of paper in his pocket with my name and number on it. She explained what had happened medically, and I suppose I was in shock or something because I didn't really take in what she was saying. She said they couldn't locate any other friends, or track down his father, that she appreciated this was a bad time, but arrangements had to be made.

I said,

"I think I'm going to have to call you back."

I buried Jimmy in the garden. I just couldn't stand the thought of him being among strangers.

I planted a hanging cherry tree over him. It fills up with birds sometimes. The singing coming out of that tree is not to be believed. There's flower beds on either side. A lot of people don't know he's there. There's no reason for them to know.

For a couple of months after, I realized I'd lost interest in life. I felt as though I were floating. Nothing seemed to connect, or make an impression. But then I said to myself,

"Lillian, enough."

I can't believe where I am sometimes. Any spare moment I can, I sit in the garden reading. Occasionally pausing to take in the sea. Right now I'm hovering somewhere between Jacqueline Susann and Grace Paley. I can feel myself opening here. I am exactly where I want to be.

Since I started serving coffee the nursery has become quite the little social spot.

She picks up the glass of water from the stool.

In warm weather I give caffeinated tours in which you walk through the greenhouses sipping a superbly prepared, even if I do say so myself, espresso or latte, while I give out background information and growing tips.

"With the right application of light, I've discovered a way of keeping chrysanthemums in bloom all year round.
They are a hardy annual, but like all plants require effort."

I wonder if we all end up where we're supposed to be.

If you lay out the incidents of our lives, they form the most exquisite poetry.

Part Seven
The Present

CHRYSANTHEMUMS (REPRISE)

Lillian is standing.

There's a man who comes 'round here.
He buys chrysanthemums from me for a store up the coast.
His name is James. Has the palest eyes.
I find myself just looking at them sometimes in disbelief.

He plays me rock music and tells bad jokes.
The other day he came over all excited.
"Lillian, I've finally got a good one.
A snail goes into a used car dealer. Says to the dealer,
'Show me the spiffiest, fastest car you have.'
The dealer points him to a Ford Mustang.
'Fine, I'll take it,' says the snail.
'No, wait a minute. Paint an S on the back.'
So the car dealer paints an S on the back of the car.
Snail looks at it, says, 'That's good. Paint an S on the front too.
The dealer obliges.
'You know what,' says the snail, 'paint an S on both sides.'
So the car dealer paints an S on both sides.
'Perfect,' says the snail.
The car dealer looks at the snail curiously,
'I hope you don't mind me asking, but why did you have me do that?'
The snail answers,
'Because when I drive down the road
I want people to say, "Look at that S car go."'"

She places the glass back on the stool.

The two of us completely lost it.

I know he's interested. He lights up, then gets all shy.
Picking out blooms. Averting his pale eyes.
But I'm taking my time. There's no rush. None at all.

> *She smiles, exuding a kind of radiance.*

I'm not going anywhere.

> *Lights fade.*

End of Play